1961

The Linen Bands

The Linen Bands

BY RAYMOND ROSELIEP

THE PREFACE BY JOHN LOGAN

THE NEWMAN PRESS · 1961 · WESTMINSTER, MD.

for my mother

Contents

Acknowledgments

America, Approach, The Beloit Poetry Journal, Best Articles & Stories, The Catholic World, Chicago Choice, Chicago Review, College Art Journal, College English, The Colorado Quarterly, The Commonweal, Compass Review, The Delta Epsilon Sigma Bulletin, Drama Critique, The English Journal, Four Quarters, Fresco, Hawk & Whippoorwill, The Indian P. E. N. (Bombay), Inscape, The Louisville Courier-Journal, The Massachusetts Review, Modern Age, Mutiny, Newman, The New Orleans Poetry Journal, Poetry (Chicago), The Poetry and Drama Magazine, Spirit, Sponsa Regis, The Tablet (London), Threshold (The Lyric Players, Inc., Belfast), The University Bookman, The University of Kansas City Review, The Waterloo Review (Ontario).

Many of these poems were recorded for Harvard University.

The Preface by John Logan first appeared in Mutiny under the title "Priest and Poet. A note on the art of Raymond Roseliep."

Preface

The priest and the poet have often combined badly. Still, many priests have loved many poets. Saint Paul quotes Aeschylus apparently with feeling. John Chrysostom was devoted to Aristophanes and they say read him daily, as Augustine did Virgil. It would be a rare priest who did not love the poet of the powerful Psalms or the author of the incomparable poem of poems, The Song of Songs, which many poets have themselves drawn on, as E. E. Cummings, or an older poet much closer to the priesthood, Saint John of the Cross, whose poems Father Martin D'Arcy so loves.

But even in the relationship of priest to poet-not-himself there has been much heat, some poets even having been made the object of official hatred and put on the Index, though it is not true, as a student once insisted to me, that Dante has had to be condemned for putting popes in his Hell.

Saint Augustine did not always respond with love to poetry. When the sadly named young student Licentius sent a poem dedicated to him, Augustine (who struggles with this same gifted college boy in the dialogue De ordine) replied after an insultingly long interval; he wrote a blistering letter denouncing Licentius as much because of the goodness of the poem as because of its shortcomings, saying the youth cared more for the laws and numbers of his work than for those of his own soul—scolding him for being more ashamed of a disordered poem than of a disordered life. "If you can't hear me when I ask you to come to God," that brilliant, terrible teacher said, "listen to your own poem. Listen to yourself, hard, cruel, deaf that you are. Where else shall I find a tongue of gold and a heart of iron? I need not your verses, but your lamentations."

In Saint Augustine we find the ultimate complication of the relations between priest and poet: we see a part of the meaning of the heat, for he loved a good poet if he was a good man, speaking in the *De musica* of how poetry excels by number, by the power of the numbering God, Who orders the organs of speech and the patterns of their sounds. And he distrusted invincibly the power of poetry itself to make a man good—on, I take it, the strongest of grounds: he himself having been a poet in his youth. He was an able one, a prize-winning one, and he never lost from his prose the ear of the poet for rhythmic cadence and for what can only be called the energy of the word.

So Augustine's quarrel with poetry was a quarrel with himself, like Plato's—the Greek philosopher also began as a poet and wrote with great, moving, paradoxical art of the need for exiling poets from his Republic.

(Ironically, when aged Socrates had begun to settle some of his own quarrels with himself, we learn from the *Phaedo*, he felt free to try a poem.)

There is a special heat between the priest and the poet when the poet in question is the priest himself. How can he not wonder whether, as people say so easily, "he would be a better priest if he were not a poet," or, "he would be a better poet if he were not a priest."

Now heat is painful. Of course artists have never minded pain so long as they could keep it from killing them and could get their work done. So long as the madman, the beast, and the angel Thomas found in himself, or the boy, the man, and the woman Joyce found in himself did not crack the china skull in which they sprouted dangerously together. Artists have been Penelopes stringing their agonies into tapestry, or Phoebes giving into the song of birds their inner violations, or Orpheuses using their torn limbs for lyres; aged Oedipuses, furious, hurt, dirty, but possessing something that makes others fight to bear them to their holy shrines. Philoctetes abiding their injuries and exile because of their great, gifted, musical bows which make them sought after despite the stink of their wounds. Achilles, bad-heeled, bad-tempered, over-mothered, melancholy but brilliant when they issue from their tents to help in the bloody inner wars men always lead, always in need of art for aid.

"Aus meine grossen Schmerzen," said Heine, one of the unhappiest of the greatest, "mach ich die kleinen Lieder."

But fame, the desire for audience, the descent of the father into creation through the word, cools the sweat of the layman wrestling with the poet in him, helps the strain of the crippled Jacob ambiguously trying to throw out from him, or to contain more comfortably, his blazing erupting angel; and I will never know how those priest-poets Robert Southwell and Gerard Hopkins calmed themselves writing not for the ears of men. Or how the poet Thomas Merton when he became Father Louis could have preferred silence, or how numbers of priest-poets are satisfied with the small applause, the minor sound, of bad religious publications, if they deserve more and do not "grate on their scrannel Pipes of wretched straw."

The art of Raymond Roseliep deserves more and has begun to get it.

The heat between the priest and poet in Father Roseliep is increased by the presence of the teacher in him. It is a difficult combination because the best priest prays most, the best poet sings loudest, and the best teacher tries to keep quiet; and because the priest can kiss closely with hands or with the breath of his mouth, the poet kisses with imagination, but the teacher can touch only with the remote idea. Father Roseliep is awfully right when he says of this triple job in his *Short Letter to Dr. Johnson*, it is "the oddest role." These three, the priest, the poet, the teacher, are held together either by mere love, which is the thinnest of threads if it's not the strongest, or by art, or by both. I think that in Father Roseliep they are held together by both.

It is easier to talk about art than about love, though every work of art is an act of love, doubly: art always makes one of two, building to the higher unity; and the artist gives in to his muse with the lover's abandon. And it is easier to talk about courage than about love. Surely Father Roseliep has courage not to have been thrown by the awful paradox faced by the poet of religious poems, who knows his readers will think him specially religious, and who is therefore hard put not to think so himself, or to take delight that they think so. The bridges are all broken across the ditch of hypocrites in the 8th circle of

xiv

Dante's Christ-quaked Hell, as though the visiting artist had necessarily to mingle with the leaden-costumed sinners there, daring the job-hazard of the religious poet. Surely it's a greater hazard for the priest-poet than for the layman?

Father Roseliep's poems fall into groups: they are poems of a younger man, or poems of a priest, or poems of a teacher, or poems from a multiple of these roles.

The Linen Bands, his most important work, is the poem of a priest. No poet not a priest could have written it. And The Unrepentant for further example goes beyond the experience of another kind of artist. Room 210: Shakespeare is the poem of the teacher. A Short Letter to Dr. Johnson goes beyond the experience of either priest-poet or teacher-poet alone, requiring both. Still other poems such as Ragman are simply the poems of a young man in whom it is difficult to find the two vocations; or a poem like Picasso's "Boy with a Pipe," one of the most beautiful of all, is the homage of the word-artist to the painter, behind which it is perhaps as hard to see the priest-teacher as it is to see the physician behind William Carlos Williams' Wedding Dance (of Brueghel) or the insurance salesman behind Wallace Stevens' Blue Guitar (of Picasso).

Still one pauses in his distinguishing—couldn't we relate the powerful, heavy motions, the gestures of every bodily member in Brueghel's painting, to the interest of the physician? Certainly the contrast of the physical immersion in that painting and the brooding detachment in Picasso's Man with a Blue Guitar can be related respectively to the whole naturalistic style of Williams as artist on the one hand and the whole introspective intellectualizing style of Stevens on the other hand—isn't it like the difference between the physician's understanding of the living (dying) body and the actuary's understanding, supposing the mastery of art in both? And in Father Roseliep's *Boy with a Pipe* we can see the uneasy love of the teacher for his young men, the anxious understanding that comes from a willingness to know their peculiar suffering and their peculiar cruelty (which so often calls forth in the older man again his own memories of pain and instincts to cruelty—tempered in this poem as by the charity of a priest). Can't we put this poem beside *Three Students, Bearing Gifts* and see the whole priest-poet-teacher behind each?

Perhaps the poems do not after all separate well into groups. They are the poems of a man-and-priest-and-teacher. *As Petrarch Coming* is the poem of love renounced in a man who became a priest. The tone of the beauty verges from that in the love poem of a poet who does not become a priest; only the suffering of the renunciation is that of any man. A poem like *Tightrope Walker*, addressed to "my young denial and/my blinded friend," is different, coming through the art of one who has given up one kind of fathering for three others: the spiritual, the intellectual, the creative.

Technically the work of Father Roseliep is ordinarily impeccable. In the careful stanzaics of an early poem like *Song of Dust* the *ababcc* rhyme scheme provides a pattern of full chime favoring the theme, with the couplet giving chance for climax, while the short, four-stress line surprises with its breadth of imagery and theological material. In the careful syllabics of a later poem like *Convent Infirmary* advantage is taken of the nine-syllable line to break down the predictable iambics of the normal English verse line (of which Roseliep shows himself master, in poem after poem): "led the virginal foot over asp/and basilisk, sweating at his work/like the yeoman's Canon." The same lines illustrate the good ear of this poet, which fails him seldom. An effective simultaneous consonance and enjambment are shown in this quotation from *Boy with Melon:* "belly protruding from unbottoned/shirt, hairless chest. . . ."

There is little free or cadenced verse in the present corpus of Roseliep's art, but he works well in blank verse and in a variety of set forms, such as the sonnet (*As Petrarch Coming*), quatrain (*Helmet* and *College Vet*), and terza rima stanza (*The Poetry Recital*), besides a number of other tightly stanzaed forms. The five-stress lines of the long, ambitious monologue *Linen Bands* follow the *abba* pattern throughout, with the second and third rhymes generally departing from the strict echo rhymes of the other two verses; this envelope scheme as a continuous form gives a curious, reflective, involuted sense to the movement. Father Roseliep handles happily the epistolary idiom of such a poem as *A Short Letter to Dr. Johnson* as well as the contemporary speech idiom of *Heels Wear Down* and the more self-consciously poetic diction of several of his pieces. Indeed, this artist gives the impression that he can write well and competently in any form and idiom he chooses. His wide craftsmanship is fit friend to Father Roseliep's long field of subjects and his good human sky of values. He is a poet to savor and one for whose future we will keep vigil.

JOHN LOGAN

Notre Dame, Indiana

The Linen Bands

THE LINEN BANDS

I did not hear the nameless angels, or
the named, attend my ordination rite,
as grade school sisters often calculate
in 2nd nocturn flights. Instead, the floor
of our cathedral sanctuary picked
a leather and a mortal sound to press
within my ear, not waiting for surprise:
a priest came up to me on heels that clicked.
He carried, as a precious cargo, bands
of linen. Though I knew the moment spelled
a symbol from our liturgy, and held
no shock, still I would notify my hands,
dozing in olive brighter than a tree.
The priest unbolted strands of white, and bound
my thumbs and fingers, like an open wound.
Thus I was tied to Christ, or Christ to me.

Today the other ceremonies dim:
the sober candle shadowing my face,
the calling of my name and how I rose,
the chanting to Augustine, Magdalen,
the Virgin, and the saints who terrify,
my body lying in a marble groove
of floor, the handing and the handling of
the instruments, a preface aimed too high,
an awful weight of hands upon my head,
the bee drone of the Latin in our Mass,
a chasuble as heavy as a cross,

my *hoc est enim corpus* firmly said.
But those are images for which I grope,
far in the mind; and if I now recall
their point and power, I seem to feel
the pull of thread as woven as a rope.

It would be poetry to open up
my store of feelings and to play a prank
with them, by saying I was wholly drunk
as an apostle on a flowing cup
of recent grape, as James perhaps, or Paul;
or that I gallivanted into night
with stars and music and a weaving gait,
as flushed as David after harping Saul.
No, rather I was like a man struck dumb,
and doomed to listen to the fountainhead
of silence. I remember how I slipped
from church to find my people who had come
to see the *miracle* (my brother's word,
exaggerated as his sudden kiss),
and how my mother wept with woman ease;
and how my hands, now free, were briefly stirred.

My hands are busy in a blessing way
since then, and they absolve and they unite,
and in our several sacraments, anoint;
they pour a water that is life. Today
I pause to wonder why they often shake

when lifting bread so light within the Mass,
or why, when sometimes touching other flesh
they want to yield: and yet they do not break.
Priest hands—ah there's the holy rub, as Will
might pun it—and I live to comprehend
the meaning underneath the stringy bond
that holds them to an unseen love, and hill.
Each time I watch a young man pray, then go,
my facile breath grows audible and tight,
and mind re-girds the will with strips of white
that have the burning quality of snow.

A SHORT LETTER TO DR. JOHNSON

To recall a conversation with Mr. Boswell,
beginning, "Sir, I love the acquaintance of
young people," and culminating with, "but
then the dogs are not so good scholars."
Turk's Head Coffee House, 22 July 1763.

Sir:
I love the young dogs of my age. They may
not love a page of solid type as I
could wish, although I plan to lead the horse
to water. But they are so tall and tan
and honest. And they show—no, give—a soul.
You see, I have the oddest role: a priest
who teaches in a school of liberal arts
and science, one who seldom preaches or
baptizes; still, I hear confessions in
and out of season; too, I bring them Shakespeare, Milton, and some other gods as you.
This is a yeoman's job. Yet I am hopeful that the dogs (poor scholars, Sir) will last
the longest as acquaintances, and far
beyond the reach of bird or star—but there!—
I do not mean to turn a foppish line or preach.

How odd that he should come for penance in
the striped Bermuda shorts. September had
been warm, and boys are boys no matter how
you find them; and perhaps the heat was getting me, I wanted very much to laugh.

The best way to discard temptation (was
it Oscar's epigraph?) is to give in.
Yet I strove hard to choke my mirth. This is
no laughing matter, I repeated like
an antiphon.
                        The eighteen years looked solemn
on the prie-dieu in my parlor, but
suppose the kneeler, at his sudden move,
should pinch uncalloused knees?

                                    I dare not grin.
Beside me bent a replica of Christ.
Though was I really willing to ignore
the buckle cap, now rolled between the legs?
God wore no cap—but then, His hair was long,
and with a butch He may have overtopped
convention.
                        Replica of Christ. And grow-
ing to the likeness more and more by aid
of my absolving hand.
                                    I raised my arm
(and Holy Ghost forgive the smile, at my

expense): a decade of a poplin sleeve
ripped at the shoulder seam. I quite forgot
a mother's warning that her needlework
insured no seamless garment, and the other Christ would need repair.

                       Amen: the Ivy
league and ragged *alter Christus*, one.

PICASSO'S "BOY WITH A PIPE"

The artist borrowed circus features from
a youth in tights, drawn earlier. A blue
hangover broods on shirt and trousers—or
had poor Picasso overbought that color
and then let it struggle with a ter-
racotta pink unruly as the flesh?
Why bicker?
                    Here's a boy with roses round
his head—and not surprised, if he should reach,
to find the stamen of the flower damp
and sticky; yet he smokes a careless pipe
to reassure the head that it can hold
a man's estate. The right arm drops and pines
and nearly points the hunger of the young.
    Flowers play in circle on the wall,—
and brow, as I have said,
                              returning me
to saltimbanque and boy and maybe god.

FROM HIS STUDY WINDOW

(Men's College)

Coral and peach were never masculine,
and so he knew the parked convertible
rephrased a lipstick or an evening gown.
He wouldn't eavesdrop, only listen well.

How silver-sweet sound lovers' tongues by night:
yet how could tyros find ambrosia
who still were bottle-fed?—although on art—
and hardly once removed from love and awe.

Behind them he could see the chapel clock
which kept the gong to centuries of doom.
This couple had no need for looking back
or for suspecting the inconstant moon.

Here played the TV lovers as unreal
as mortal puppets they had tried to ape.
Fearing his truer Romeo should pale,
he closed the window and his text, for sleep.

In morning lecture he would prime his men
on love a printed page can wall secure.
Plotting to make his hero breathe again,
he felt the slamming of a coral door.

Check-in, the thud upstairs, a faucet, cough—
the dormitory would be quiet soon.
And he must dream a wiser book's belief,
or hear the bells of bones clang in their tomb.

THREE STUDENTS, BEARING GIFTS

Be mery and not sad;/of myrth is oure sang.

   . . . Prophetys haue spokyn:
To so poore as we ar/that he wold appere,
Fyrst fynd, and declare/by his messyngere.
    The Second Shepherds' Play, Towneley cycle

In parka, GI jacket, split-tail tweed,
the shepherds come to usher in Noël.
The Towneley rustics donned no gayer garb
to wrap their cherries, bird, and tennis ball.

I spread potato chips and cokes as foils
to college fare, detach the holly seal
while half afraid that I should muff my cue
and tremble like a lover or a fool.

A super-grain Kaywoodie, and pre-smoked,
a Ronson—never fails, and balks the wind,
a shirt, monsignor red, for partying:
their trinity of splendor stings my hand.

December lowers, and I light a lamp
much in the way I would switch on a star,
but no one hundred fifty watts will tell
that it is I who am the wanderer.

Though sky and cloud are voicing bitterness
against the outside (or the inside) wall,
we chat of bowling scores, of ski jumps cleared,
the softball future, Shakespeare's staring owl.

And thanks for all your presents, merry men;
pull up your monk's hood, Jim—that sleet is wild.
I'll bask in flame of lighter, pipe, and shirt
(but not until I find, and gift, the Child).

THE POETRY RECITAL

(for John Logan*)

He tuned the Andes with Chicago's saint
like a thrush outbalancing its neck
of windpipe, perilous to limb and joint.

In Cumbre air where every breath rang thick
and vowel thin as wing or hyaline,
his sweatdrops oozed into a cheekbone crock.

The ear reached up and caught a fingering
of keys that freed the melody he now
remembered from a stanza rhyming lean.

No flowing he had ever heard could tow
a music keen as this: to pare the flesh
and make a man more naked in his awe.

He shivered to an interval of hush
among his students at the mountain foot,
afraid that some saw ember snuff to ash.

But heirloom seconds of his Elgin flicked
away the silence. As he chimed a page
of frightened bells within his manuscript

*reading "Mother Cabrini Crosses the Andes," from his
Cycle for Mother Cabrini

to round Francesca's cycle or to dodge
a self of incomplete, arriving moon,
ribs told they had fulfilled a mountain urge.

Descending, he surmised he should go home,
slip through the gateway of his private yard,
and for the length of starcount be alone.

Secure inside, he could rake up the shard.

THE UNREPENTANT

In lime green shirt, italicizing fad,
he eased onto a grill of leather chair.
The priest could smell the paler ghost of beer
that sometimes pinches any man (or lad)

who dreams of quieting his conscience gong.
No matter. Sprawled was six-feet-one of frame
casking a thirst that craved a sharper foam
than ever tantalized his lips or tongue.

Although he planned to hide the flimsy tear,
which he protested was a gift for girls,
he had not guessed or gambled how some oils
upon an apostolic hand would glare

into a sea of self, and flame to strike
an enemy not ready to disband.
His crying was no jag: for once, he found
a balm less parching than his inward ache.

The priest was pouring dross into his ear:
about Augustine and the world it took
before his conscience belled a last rebuke.
The boy had shifted in the sticky chair,

and felt its leather brand his flesh: *Not yet.*
Along his backbone perspiration ran
cool lime. He saw himself a full grown man
for whom the taller sinner must have wept.

ROOM 210: SHAKESPEARE

Front row, and parked at 9:00: the denim taut
on either leg to stress the muscle flow;
arms bare and gnarled as branches—and one thought
of Adam limbed by Michelangelo.

In form and moving how express. And yet
he never scooped my pearls into his *notes*,
or laughed (in courtesy) at jokes inset
as bribes to yawners needing antidotes.

In apprehension—but how could *he* share
that portion of the *piece of work?* His skull
lay buried in a richer head of hair;
the gridiron paid his college bills in full.

*The beauty of the world, the paragon
of animals*: no one would dare dispute
the niche he filled by right as Adam's son
—though beautiful *in se* is every brute.

How like an angel . . . but another gong
must wake, and he will straighten to adjust
his creeping shorts, then rise and join a throng
of bodies boned of quintessential dust.

PROFESSOR NOCTURNAL

Now Air is hush'd, save where the weak-ey'd Bat,
With short shrill Shriek flits by on leathern Wing. . . .
                    Collins, *Ode to Evening*

> Dismissing bees and bookmen from
> *The Grumbling Hive,*
> he pads in April dusk, afraid
> to be alive.
>
> He cannot weather crew-cut flings
> at gaiety,
> but only nod, unlatch a smile,
> and grieve that he
>
> (who all his students claim is wise
> as Solomon)
> should dread the silly hiding of
> the aging sun.
>
> Near bat-time, to the safe indoors,
> where lamb chops warm,
> he hurries from his boyhood spectres
> of alarm.
>
> Brandied and lounged, he slackens fear
> at pages numb
> with Congreve jabs—till midnight-
> punctual, THEY come.
>
> Bats loop from Collins' evening ode
> on the calm shelf,
> rip the planks his brier smoked
> about a self;

slosh the floating
freckles pale,
whimper for blood,
lift hair to nail;

snap, dive,
icicle bone
and the pump
in the chest zone;

squeak warnings of
a gloomier hole
than terra firma
to his soul.

Bed will be bitter,
tangly, damp,
small solace wick
his all-night lamp.

He bargains the Lord
his soul to keep.
But what if he start
eternal sleep,

caught at last
in a web of wing,
bit, sucked
by a blacker Thing?

PORTRAIT OF A PHILOSOPHER

I think, by way of compromise and convenience, I shall call
him the Scarabee. He has come to look wonderfully like
those creatures,—the beetles, I mean,—by being so much
among them.

He is an enthusiast . . . he is never content except when
he is making somebody uncomfortable. He does certainly
know one thing well, very likely better than anyone in the
world.

[But there are] two sides to everybody. . . .
The Poet at the Breakfast-Table

Like Thomas Sawyer, & ahem, he made
goldleaf distinctions for us ably. Spades
were never ever spades, and so we felt
he really ought to hide in Plato's cave,
for language DID conceal his thought, and his
philosophy COULD split the atom of
a ghost, or part of its anatomy
at most.

The Scarabee we dubbed him se-
cretly in frat (then downed a toast to Holmes,
and not at breakfast table either): for
the imposition of a high-flown ride
was his obsession. He'd get on our backs
and brandish breeze until we wished J. Keats

was wrong about that Shelley-aery sword:
an angel's wing could be—indeed was—clipped!

Denying majors gave him mediae-
val glee, though he was in the minor league.
Behind a Scotch, we did not mind so much
his pitch from artful Aristotle to
the sinless Santayana (died in Rome);
and more than once we wanted to pronounce
an *existentialism* he could spurt
without a stutter; but, "O Pharisees,"
he'd mutter, and we'd keep complacency.

A "Pish" would quiet us on Women (lovely sport) for None threw metaphysical
softballs or swung bats cosmological—
the switch was marvelous: one game he claimed
he never played, yet dared to referee!
(I should not mention very loud that on
his face we saw the slightest greyish cloud.)

He left as suddenly as he had come.
Had mumbled something of a work not done;
a private biz, he said, we'd never dig;
some nasty job he must attend alone;
and it would pluck the heart out of a year;
still we should meet again somehow, but not
till he had killed a grey and little fear.

The girl had asked a simple question: how
to hide her feelings and still win the boy.
Her head was in a whirl, and she was ill
from loving. Bachelor of hearts, I'd have
the answer.
    Yes, of sorts.
        Pretend you love
another—rather—and be vague as fog.
The snake will rear its ugly head and wake
the lamb, or maybe man. A fleece of sound
will tickle on your ear before too long.

How easily I poured my balm into
the wound of waiting; and I felt it heal.

I'm not of many words, but thank you (well
she used her *Much Ado*).
       Don't mention it.

Now she must go. She put her flower hand
in mine and said I was divine and wished
I weren't so old as forty [sic] or she'd
be sold on me perhaps.
      Goodnight, my girl.
These freshman themes depend upon a midnight oil.
   . . my dear.
      (The bluer pencil lines
will make me wonder whether you could guess
a middle-aged professor's wistfulness.)

FOR A YOUNG MAN, OUT OF LOVE

Now you are "out of love," your letter states,
at early twenty-one (and I would laugh
if laughter didn't seem a sacrilege
on ground so solemn). Dryden had a word:
woman!/Dear, damned, inconstant sex!—you must
recall it from our drama course? and how
I pointed up the dear and told you of
the room in everyman for woman's light
to bless, and in his darks a need of her
pressed flower tenderness. Or going back
to this: how rough men bruise as Lazarus
when first awake, and how they start when woman
makes her presence felt as though she were
a wand of light about to break.

                        So, all
for love, my sprout and upstart. It may take
a year of aprils with their moons. But wait.
A brightness will remove your vigil when
that lady, lovely in her station, comes:
to want your arms and all your spirit holds
for holiness.
                (Your old professor did
not find this answer in a play or poem;
and although today his mind is married
to a book, it never will forget
a broken stick of light that fell across
his single pathway.)

Woman is the fire
and fibre of your man's existence, as
the elements of its philosophy.
Be patient and be lonely in your nights,
remembering a woman also waits.

COLLEGE VET
(*locker room*)

"The beanpole's back," they cheered, "and *reely* whipped";
"he sure got caught in Uncle Sammy's draft";
"hey, Shoulders, want some pads?" The GI stripped:
to wounds that narrowed life. And no one laughed.

THE MISOGYNISTS

The students, puzzled that a gal would stew
some eels in broth to duck a handsome boy,
felt sorry for the lad who could not go
out hunting any more. One said, "A guy

can't have his private fun—a skirt will spoil
it"; and another moaned, "No fem is kind
by nature." So they all condemned the girl,
but left Lord Randal's mother undefined.

ENTER BACHELOR PROF WITH UKE

He brought a ukulele to his class,
played from a poet not immortal:
about a sailor and his faithless lass,
and why the swabby downed a bottle.

He warbled sad as Keats's nightingale:
"The poor fish cut her heart asunder";
when "No one budged to raise the lubber's bail,"
he wept, and made his students wonder.

24

HELMET

Place, O Lord, on my head the helmet of salvation,
that I may be armed against the attacks of the enemy.

Prayer: in rubric for priest, vesting

Irreverence was not my aim,
but amice touched my head like sun:
the Methodists fought Notre Dame.
7–6. The Irish won.

LIKE SEASON, LIKE STUDENT

September, they punt and tackle and plunge
past pages uncut;
but even a prof may read himself
into a rut.

December, it's leaps for basketed space,
though footnotes don't jump,
and satcheled schoolboys creep like snails.
Ho, chest! down, thump!

Come March, whose pitch? who's up to bat?
The print will not rot.
What bard was an umpire? or, Was one?
I forgot.

June with a "Fore!" drowns Tennyson's "Break!"—
and exams fall next.
Students behind on their scores, see me.
Now, the text . . .

25

GRADUATE

Check gear of gown,
tackle of hood,
mortarboard trim
—Lord it is good.

Signal the frigates
docked on the stage.
Warn the mind's deck
to rage against rage.

Cut parchment surf,
softer than satin,
shattering wide
the rockfast Latin.

Sweep the sea
of naughty night,
plow, little dreadnought,
wink your light.

EPISTLE TO E. E.

if your song world is a trifle bent
as you have confessed more than a sing-
able sonnet ago, and flashwing
season of spring is giving no hint
of one particular flowing throat
(created for a poet's question
by the lightmaker who can rest on
his laurels, unwaiting the same note),

then, dear mister e. e. cummings, why
not apply simply with an upstroke
of your best vocal breath to the head
of the firm(ament)? and he may play
a little super natural joke
and fly you the hopkins Bird instead.

ON SPRAWLING EARTH

Saturday afternoon sprawls over
the country land he picks for kingdom,
blue circled and crowned with the sweet pear:
from the ground he watches the bough loom
into the light of the driven jay,
—though his thin socked ankles must revel
in the tickling feel of the stubble,
and his tongue relish a blade of hay.

His eye follows the transcending bird
carrying the light away from him.
Now the branches look sullen and wild.
But he is young in pride and no word
of his will motion the dark fruit down
where earth is foothold of man-and-child.

BOY WITH MELON

The world circling is indifferent
to his melon full face, wonderful
belly protruding from unbuttoned
shirt, hairless chest, Murillo-head deep
in hair. And the boy doesn't much care
so long as hard rind throbs when he rolls
his thumb, testing before the lonely
errand of blade summon the honey.
He sees a moment of spray shower
his trouserleg, pouts, and returns to
the joy in discovering a life
that ripens elusively under
largelidded eyes reviewing the nails
of his own right hand, sweet as the knife.

A IS FOR APOLLO

Pain that is not yet the pain of love
anchors his manframe. He lies goldskinned
and handsome on the stones, attentive
to whatever stirrings of the pond
he is refavoring from boyhood:
the water rilling over his chest
and ribs and over the slightly awed
loins of the boy that are curving wist-
fully to their twentieth sea change.
He tilts a wetgold head to the bank
where his eyes half close upon a fringe
of fern letting in delicate pink
skycolor and a tincture of sun
or the girl suddenly the woman.

WHERE ROOTS TANGLE

Where roots tangle the ground before their plunge
under, he hooks his heels. His backbone rests
keenly against the oak as the sun sets,
making his faded sweater more like orange.
His face reaches for chinks of light between
the leaves so he can time the moment day
is an equation with his fires that die,
and substitute a colder twig of moon.

The boy of love is moping while that hill
becomes a shadowgraph. But he must turn
from his esthetic distances almost
as sharply as he taught them to his will
once he discovers roots lead down and burn.
And he will mark the night, this light-heeled ghost.

RECOMMENDATION:
IN STILL-EARLY SPRING

A history of love has blossomed
and died for a night in him.
As the dry corn tossed
he is coming,
bringing for his credential
himself and a newer longing
to the field of your early spring.

Dark is the lover coming
for exquisite burial
carrying the whirl
of brightgreen.

Be soil and sun and woman
when you see him lean
to the acres of your marvelous spring.

A history of love will tassel
greenbrightly in your land
from end to delicate end,
and death be blown to symbol.

The soul in the corn is humming
while the flesh on the corn is dim:
Young is the lover coming.
Love him.

TONIGHT, A MIRACLE OF AIR

Tonight, a miracle of air
you touch my dead grove
and the branches move
with excellent fire.

You sing in their marrow bone
holier passion
and sing a dimension
where ravens have flown.

I have loved you enough
for a night: and well
may the flaming apple
fall on my father's roof.

THE LATELY LOVED

You float among my books and smoky room
pulling our distance near, and you distract
music-for-reading with a dainty art
of Ariel whipping the air to foam.
Dew light and colorless as spirit light
you flit beyond the sea reach of my arms,
behaving like a wisp of borrowed bait
a Prospero might dangle to the forms
that swim the dry land or a young man's dream.
You swirl and trick my lutanist, and gnarl
the airy lines, dipping to see me grieve
splash-twinkled out of volume heavy time
—a peril and a disembodied girl
who take a man unguarded in his love.

DANSE MACABRE

The young make love along a bank of river.
But in the spilt geography I trace
a lively rite, giving a name and face
to what I visited and 'vowed' forever.
They are all here, the fierce and the lovely,
sporting their shrouds of fashionable grey,
the bony driftwood clinging to the clay;
a lovetime older and dancing darkly.

Higher upon the river bank the young
laugh down to me. But I am drawn by
the dancers and should never glance over
my shoulder to be trapped by other song,
who am appointed fiddler of the day,
grieving a little for the intense lover.

ANNIVERSARY

I had forgotten you and all your ways,
had breathed a Tuscan air and called it pure,
feeling so sacramental and secure
a decade of three hundred fifty days.
I never counted, to my own surprise,
how much a clock would spend to buy a year,
and laughed out loneliness or laughed down fear.
Tonight is different, and Dante lies.

I separate the minutes now like sands—
the poet's sublimation is a joke.
A woman is the tangible of light
—the way she curves her mouth or moves her hands:
I do remember, love. But Dante spoke
to shove his grief to universal height.

AS PETRARCH COMING

Benedetto sia 'l giorno e 'l mese e l'anno . . .
                    Rime, I, sonetto xxxix

As Petrarch coming with a laurel wreath
to living Laura, blessing bow and day,
I too approach an anniversary
and trim the votive candle of my faith:

alive, and you are dead to me. I wrote
renouncement on your stone. Now, bravery
has tolled to summon all the man in me.
I kneel no longer in my boyhood myth.

The faulty wisdom of a youth who loved
will somehow brim, as mine, into a thirst
which moves him as no christ was ever moved,

to down the sponge of gall because he must.
And it is right, as other love has proved.
I give this Whitman lilac to your dust.

SOME MEN A FORWARD MOTION LOVE

"Still haven't finished childhood" was the clause
that closed his letter; then he added, "In
more ways than one." By childhood he had meant
those Joycean trips through alleys of the mind
I beg to leave unlanterned. He explains,
it takes a child to catch a child: and swears
by it. I do not tell him I am more
the usual coward who transfers a fear.
This lighting back perturbs me like the search
through darkness for a blacker cat not there.
Let midnight wicks inform a virgin's fool-
ish wait, or scholar's watch. My friend is I,
and I'm afraid of I, and want no back-
ward steps. Childhood is over, and we shove
ourselves to manhood, linking arm with those
who feign a forward motion, or we move
from shadow into shadow, not from love.

TO A YOUNG LADY, AGE FOUR,
WHO ASKED TO MARRY ME

I have dallied with your proposal,
dear Elizabeth, and would prefer
a little more time to consider
since four to forty is, after all,
a bit of a distance . . and eighteen
to fifty-four touches grave matter.
Till the present oat flower has gone
from your very yellow hair, and I
have tended to the mulberry sky
that has persistently overrun
its color, and even courtesy,
in either hopeful, questioning eye,
may I remain your affectionate
friend, dear, and (lonelier) laureate.

TO JIM / ON GOING TO THE WARS

What does a man say to a man, at last?
Nice knowing you. So long. Good luck and keep
your shirttail clean.
                    Cry in our beer. And soak
the pillowcase tonight and night to follow, weep. For "warriors' tears are the strong sil-
ver things": a poet not a pantywaist
proclaimed it—David's Jonathan or Burns
I think.
            Good by. Go to the wars, profess
their honor, and love honor less.
                                    I'll see
you in the morning. Buddy.
                                Leave the mush-
room by the ocean; only bring a shell
to sing your voyage in my ear . . or send
it for a dogtag and I'll learn the cry
by heart before you (possibly) return.

THE FRIEND

We drove until the maples pointed how
the river was an autumn older too.

We stood beside the river:
                              not as boys
but men who looked for answers to the love
that neither had. He talked about the gulls,
stone faced and hungry, and although I felt
his want, I could not give even a child's
attachment to his need.

                              I dived into
my soul, disturbing relics of those others
who had swum when friendship was a word
like god
              (for then my christ was Midas who
              could make the spirit gold, and I had welcomed
              brilliance till I burned with it and learned
              the trick of drowning shadow from that reach);
and there I kicked the almost emptiness
and licked at dark. I left my soul
                              and ran
a reel of river past his eye and said:
The water is a friendly place, but notice
how that slender gull dips gracefully
to touch a surface he will never probe.

The picture hurt his eye, and he seemed fearful
that the symbols would explode before
the riddle of my hand.

                        I shook my keys.
And he was ready to be driven back
to ordinary rounds and search the oldest
corners of our towns from end to end,
having found a little less than friend.

Michigan Blvd. at 6:00 is risk-
y, but he left the walk to hail a cab,
and sparks undid the cold november curb.

Too much Picasso had me swaying, and
I shivered as we rode to catch a drink
"somewhere within an English otherworld"
because he liked a far-off atmosphere.

Pineapple soaking in a rum, the almond,
and the never bitter raisin sauce
pampered the tongue, and we talked poetry,
and were not once ashamed as men: outrun-
ning beauty and without a frequent soul
to bargain with.

          I thought it rather strange,
however, he should be annoyed that I
had sermonized how stars came from his shoes
and broke the night. He found a deeper vein
beneath my careless parable than I
had counted on.
          "Just cleats," he said, "my heels
wear down too fast." He had the master's knack
of flattening with words.
          "And so does ale—
shrimp curry—and the spirit" (now I felt
my way into the homily).

                              "Let's not
have God tonight." He dulled my pulpit plan.
Then looked at me and spoke with louder eyes
than voices from Picasso.
                              Paid the check.

And hailed another cab which brought us to
a public reading of his poems: not
so bright as sparks that briefly warmed or died
along the curb.

THE MAN WHO GRIEVED FOR GOD

At last, my Christ has gone to bed:
he sprang the catchword since he bled
the berry on our thorn of truth.
Allowing some leftover pain
which haunted him, and would again,
he shrouded his anemic youth.

With Christ so tired and so asleep,
now he could fret, or even weep
as sometimes tougher men will do;
he could revise theology
a little, though eternity
was still a primer for review.

But glossing God was his mistake
which grazed the bones and made them shake.
At most a fly-by-night relief
was all the intellect dare claim
in awkwardly engrafting shame
that rotted to a husk of grief.

With Christ unstirring, night was long
as wintertime, and bare of song.
The sounds were sharp enough to slice
a door, and he could set no lock
to stem the triple-crowing cock
or hush a soldier's clacking dice.

In shadow he must try to hide
(though Christ might toss against his side).
He troubled no one with his sighs,
but when a cracking lance of breath
suggested his (or God's) own death
he chilled, and almost said, Arise.

TIGHTROPE WALKER

You scolded Frost for boasting he had sought
forgiveness of the Lord for little jokes
he played on God, and he'd forgive the Lord
His bigger joke on Robert.
                              Then you walked
across your tightrope, and I saw you fall.

My poor psychologist unsteady as
the feet that struggle; ready to condemn
the other who is you again:
                              shake off
the sawdust and retake your step. A ring
of us are watching. Though a ring won't mind,
a friend will. Find him on a single hand
and still count fingers left.
                              The plaudit is
my faintest effort to be brave or have
a faith in you, my young denial and
my blinded friend.

                              While you and God play blind-
man's buff on what restricted cable, I
regard your turn (less eager than my love).
There's nothing funny in this business of
a searching out, and God is not your prank-
ster though He puts *His* metaphysics in
the sport.
                Go walk the fibre taut as truth
and pity all the bobbie frosts enroute
on thinner rope. Yours is the absolute.

SILENCE IS A MEAL

Homme, pèse ton poids calculé en froment.
                    St. -John Perse, *Anabase*, VIII

I thought I would run out to greet him when
he came to eat my bread again, or laugh
and loop a ring around his finger. Odd
how time can treat you, flogging joy tomorrows
hinted for this coming, and without
a warning of a change: there cannot be
a flourish or hurrahing when you meet
a figure quiet as a coal unlit.
Thus he returned today, my brother and
a stranger.

      Silence is a meal we seldom
took together; now I wonder whether
silence fills our emptiness too full.
We crack a common bread, no louder than
Isaiah looking for his lord across
the India paper of a family book.
I want to peer inside this visitor
and question if the chaff on wind, or grain-
field thinned beyond our ancient house, have made
a difference in bread. But I will notice
later when we have to weigh our weight
in terms of wheat.

The linen cover draws
some glowing from the candles to our table
catching crumbs of finished bread. The wine
cup swims another light. And we are having
supper as we did.

THE YELLOW CHRIST

"Is that Gauguin himself going over
the wall or fence behind the yellow Christ?
Why does he show only one leg on all
his straddlers—take that oil with all the horsemen—
are they symbols?"

             I had not remembered
the one-legged riders, so taken
had I been with the departing man
before me. But the questions were as honest
as the bright limbed boy who asked them (though
he could have mentioned pilfering of citron,
jonquil or the sun that lend a wayside
figure eloquence). I cleared my throat.
Then wondered (to prevent its light) what stirred
in the unconscious dark. I pared my answers.
"No, I hardly think Gauguin would mean
himself—the form is indistinct.
                    One foot
is over: that could show the man had thought
of leaving Christ behind;
                   the other one
is on this side . . and though it seems about
to scale the wall, the toes are touching ground."

"A kind of clinging to both worlds?"

                           "A kind
of, yes."

We crossed the room to see the horsemen
I had missed. I hoped he would not ask
about the yellow pigment on my back,
the streak of it along my black serge leg.

He led.
                And I was halfway in his world.

MAN AT A PICASSO EXHIBIT

An art institute is not where one expects
a lot of children, but the afternoon
he went to find Picasso in Chicago
children huddled near a portrait, scene,
abstraction, or in squares the nun with her
imaginary chalk had drawn for them.
Not wishing that the Sister see him stare,
he lowered eyes less virginal, and stale.
His body was a thing unbeautiful:
his boyhood loins were loveless in "unworthy
manhood" (what was there about that Byron
who could give a candle double flame,
then publicly make music of his skill?).
He thumbed his guidebook as he felt the knowing
smiles or heated whispers near the picture
of the naked boy leading a horse.

The children straightened when the nun explained
how an artist must arrange a body in
its simplest form—to catch the line of bone,
rounding of muscle on it, rhythm in
the arms and shoulder sweep, the hips, the legs—
"before a shirt and trousers can be fitted
on a masterpiece that God first made."

"Now, children, there's the boy again." She pointed
at a tumbler, gaudy in his diamond
patterned suit.

And children, bobbing, clean,
and fully clothed, went past the idle pages
of a guidebook and a naked man
they did not notice.

CONVENT INFIRMARY

The nun was blind as fear. She rattled
in her throat, and at her cocoa beads.
The priest who helped get her debt settled
called loudly against the noonday raids
of spear and horn, the business by dark,
led the virginal foot over asp
and basilisk, sweating at his work
like the yeoman's Canon. When the crisp
bell shoving the starched community
to compline broke to dribbling water
sound, the priest hoped someone would intone
the nightsong strong enough to matter
now and make it easier to die,
though light become a plummeting stone.

Jesus of Nazareth is going by.
No. Gone. Peter is croaking upside down
upon his cross. Stephen is groaning
underneath the stony earth. Sebastian stirs
with every arrow of my wakefulness.
The antiseptic clock has stopped, and pain
and I are stuck as roommates for the night.
Nurse, pull this rubber padding tighter. Thanks.
It's soothing to an innocence—the sheet
of heat. Joan blushes at the stake, grows black,
lets out a woman's cry; can't even die.
Saul falls, gets blinder than Picasso's old
guitar man: that's when light can really hurt.
Let Him increase, and me decrease, later:
Augustine could have yelled it—well, did,
in fact. That needle wears off too fast;
nurse, could I have another, and some ice?
my pillow's wet, what time is morning? and
this pack of cigarettes is sweating. Why's
that candle burning by the Sacred Heart?
I don't remember Sister Rita lighting
one. That nun is quite a character.
Always stewing about the rest of us.
Arthritic. Like a saint. What's a saint?
The body in its chamber reeking? Where's
the good, though, in stinking like a death,
alone and lonelier than hell? Sister
or earlier or any saint all smell.
The living dead. I feel their joining breath.
Jesus of Nazareth——

TO DR. JOHNSON,
TIDYING HIS LIBRARY

On Wednesday, April 3, in the morning I found him
busy putting his books in order . . .

You must have been a sight, if Boswell can
be accurate for once: in morning light
brushing a crowd of books until the air
is loud with dust; and Hodge the cat (my own
detail) eying the slighted quill within
a well of ink so spillable; and then
the hedger's glove sprucing the bearers of
an older wisdom, and your certain love.

Time is untidy though, and books, however
lined along the walls, will not outshine
the mind that grapples with them—Sir, I'd sooner
have you sitting there and reading; doesn't
dusting better fit a woman's hand?
But then, you had a plan I'm fairly sure:
getting the house in order, touching one
more life or two before another visitor
would lift the knocker on your door.

Snow is snowing by my church
gravely all day,
under the narrow arch
there are no prayers to pray.

Dark will fall, and faithfully
some birds will gather
in the doorway
from the cold, my brother.

I could burn a lamp
before the Virgin, with
as little pomp
as when you left;

or bow a faithless knee
in honor of the dead:
then have them naming me
our mother's renegade.

Snow is snowing by my church
wordless toward night.
Wind has a slower speech,
binding and tight:

the *Requiescat* can
be yours, and mine as well,
a word no plainer than
the choking of a bell.

FOR A SEVENTY FIFTH BIRTHDAY

Against the night my world will feather-
shake when the last breath of you has dropped
its syllable on me, my mother,
and you will be younger than I hoped,

I come running with berry buckets
damp from woodgrass and the passed meadow,
a pocketful of active crickets,
and a myth about them to read you:

a son is a boy is an ocean
of wine stored in soils of his loving;
a manchild is the child in motion
faster than a field song caught and sung.

I come leaping against the structure
of Novembers shortening the years,
at your table become a fixture
where candles in a diamond pierce.

THE DAY MY FATHER WAS BURIED

My father died and I said part of me
is dead. I peeled some willow twigs. Until
I saw a tanager streaking our grass
with fire. And I wanted to shout indoors
and tell my mother all about it and
undo the darkness at our supper hour.
But death is quiet like the kitchen or
my mother's eyes, so I would not disturb
the still life of her house.

                    On the porch I
brooded, and lost my appetite. Until
I was again distracted . . .
                       And I would
not mention at the table that I felt
all right—lest I upset my mother's sol-
itude or call attention to the lack
she must have known just then—
                          though I had seen
a bluejay with the sky upon his back.

RAGMAN

The hoofbeat down the raveled tar
came thudding softly on my ear,
though I was young to understand
my father's wonder at my fear.

On bookland trails no chariot
or prince I met rode so forlorn;
and as he blew a bugle note
I heard, within, another horn.

But when he swept me near his side
his shabbiness began to shine:
and patches glowing braided gold
surprised my half-awakened spine.

Across what worlds we drove, alive
to each incision of the rain;
the orphan wind did not ignore
our fellowship of splendid pain.

Now I am older, still I clutch
my rags of fatherless distress
and climb a golden coach to share
a loneliness with loneliness.

THE SCISSORS GRINDER

The scissors grinder belled the street
of our moping town,
and in me somersaults of dread
cramped upside down.

My mother used to coax me out
with our sluggish ware;
he singed me by his bristly touch
and razored glare.

Plying hand and eye, he ground
—my flesh was on that stone:
as he cut, the jagged sparks
seared the bone;

and at my feet in fiery pools
splinters winced and bled.
But when he iced my palms with steel
I fled, I fled.

I know I shall remember
until the night I die
the grindstone of a hairy hand,
the blade of an eye.

OVER ELEMENTS

Now that I have surrendered, God (who
would not to your tameless cry? though they
call you a lamb), and the victory
over gusty elements that go
into the making of this manshape
gathers peace not constructed by hand,
and we have joined in a common bond . .

I must endeavor simply to grope
for the figures a child will shower
naming the giver and gift, or find
a word in the Canticle lover
to rally the gentle air and bring
from the brain's own shelter the lion
out of the house of Juda roaring.

SONG OF DUST*

When four last winds have quieted
and dust has lulled the trumpeter,
when bones rewarm the flesh they shed
and wounds unlock to golden myrrh:
with senses edged and glistening,
impassibility I sing.

Lifting beyond the aeriforms
I dreamed or thought I dreamed on earth,
gliding, ethereal, by storms
that thickened from my troubled birth,
piercing the doorless wall, in place:
I sing of subtlety in space.

No lark that ever served the lean
and strict geometry of love
could cut a quicker trail, unseen,
than brother body, timed, above:
where joy has circumscribed a throng
agility obeys my song.

When skin refracts the dazzling gem
and glory of my reckoning,
when *facies ad faciem*,
as brave as other saints I sing:
of clarity retracting night,
of dust the synonym of light.

*after Thomas Aquinas, *Summa theologica*, III Suppl., q. 82–85

A NOTE ON THE TYPE

IN WHICH THIS BOOK WAS SET

This book has been set in Electra, a type face created in 1935 by W. A. Dwiggins, the well-known Boston artist. This type falls within the "modern" family of type styles, but was drawn to avoid the extreme contrast between "thick and thin" elements that marks most "modern" type faces. The design is not based upon any traditional model, and is not an attempt to revive or to reconstruct any historic type. Since its birth, Electra has met with success because of its easy-to-read quality. This book was composed and printed by the York Composition Company, Inc., of York, Pa., and bound by Moore and Company of Baltimore, Md. The design and typography of this book are by Howard N. King.